P9-DVV-609

The Nature of Wisdom

Bruce W. Heinemann

Bruce W. Heinemann

THE WISDOM OF NATURE

SPEAKS TO US HEART TO HEART,

AND NATURE'S FIRST LANGUAGE

IS BEAUTY.

· TIM MCNULTY ·

The Nature of Wisdom

INSPIRATIONS FROM THE NATURAL WORLD

Photography by Bruce W. Heinemann

Forward by Tim McNulty

Prior Publishing

Anacortes, Washington

ACKNOWLEDGMENTS

The publisher is grateful for permission to reproduce copyrighted material. While every effort has been made to trace copyright holders, the publisher would be pleased to hear from any not here acknowledged. From The Prophet by Kahlil Gibran, copyright 1923 by Kahlil Gibran and renewed 1951 by Administrators C.T.A. of Kahlil Gibran Estate and Mary G. Gibran. Used by permission of Alfred A. Knopf, a division of Random House, Inc.

Publication Date: September 15, 2005

Book design by CMYKate Designs / Kate Rappé

Printed by Premier Graphics, Bellingham, Washington

Published by:
Prior Publishing
1520 34th St.
Anacortes, Washington 98221

For Inquiries, please contact Bruce W. Heinemann
(360)588-8188
info@theartofnature.com

www.theartofnature.com

CONTENTS

THE WISDOM OF TREES

More than thirty-five years have passed since my first encounter with those grand ancient beings that grace the western shore of our continent, the coast redwoods. I was an unseasoned traveler at the time, a fledgling pilgrim if truth be told. I had stolen a month away from my college summer job in the East to journey to the golden coast of California. I'm not at all sure what I hoped to find, but my experience in the redwoods remains as fresh and vivid as this morning's rain.

A boyhood spent exploring the woods and streams around my small Connecticut town and a youthful passion for books had channeled me into a major in English. I knew I wanted to write one day. And I knew that my experiences in nature prompted deep feelings I hoped to somehow articulate. My reading of poets from the West Coast stirred a desire to visit their landscapes: the wild California coast of Robinson Jeffers, the lake-studded meadows of Kenneth Rexroth's Sierra, the misty Northwest coastline Theodore Roethke so eloquently evoked.

These and other writers left the trodden paths of academic verse and found inspiration and transcendence in the natural world. I found their poems deeply moving, and I supposed, innocently enough, that if I visited some of those same places I might share their insights.

I was inspired, to be sure, if less than enlightened. Then, hitchhiking along the northern coast, I found myself alone one evening in a magnificent grove of redwoods.

In my memory the world is green and hushed. Late sunlight slants through the canopy and a lingering shaft of light illumines the small white flowers of oxalis and sharpens the fronds of sword fern. Rhododendron blossoms fallen along the trailside glow faintly among the mosses and ferns. Above them, in dappled shadows, stand the furled, cinnamon-brown and fire-charred columns of trees. Great, burley walls of wood impossibly tall, they lift out of the forest floor as if the earth meant to shore up the sky. With barely a taper they rise to a distant canopy of splintered blue-green panes of sky, as intricate as cathedral windows.

I was struck by the centuries held in their stillness, imagining countless seasons of summer fog and winter storms passing through them like days. And the centuries too in the down hulks of fallen trees, grown over with with beds of moss and shrubs, new seedlings sprouting from their bark, the fallen petals beside them.

Then something happened. My sense of time collapsed. I felt myself expand beyond the moment of my existence. Suddenly, I saw the forest itself as a blossom, delicate and ephemeral as the small oxalis at my feet. I sensed the world as a momentary spring in which life bloomed in the warmth of its season. Not large and everlasting as the great trees might suggest, but small and precious in the immensity of the universe, delicate as a forest flower. And like the forest before me, it brimmed with unfathomable mystery and beauty.

I was barely twenty at the time, and the realization was both profound and energizing. It put many of the thoughts I had been grappling with over the past year in a bright and compelling perspective. And it strengthened my resolve to follow my instincts and pursue beauty, meaning and inspiration in nature, where I found them most readily at hand. Though there was still a year or two of school ahead of me, the great trees helped set the course of my life. Becoming the embodiment of something I must have always known, the redwoods shared their wisdom.

* * *

Humankind's traditions are rich with stories of individuals seeking meaning and wisdom in the natural world. The great prophets and visionaries of the world's religions sought wisdom in nature, often alone, apart from their human counterparts: Lao-tzu by his flowing stream in Ch'u, Jesus on the Mount of Olives, Gautama Buddha beneath his bo tree at Bodh Gaya, Mohammed on Mount Hira. It must be an ancient impulse. From Moses's sojourn on Mount Sinai to Wordswoth's walks in the Lakes District or the revelations of America's astronauts first seeing earth from the immensity of space, our visionaries have "come down from the mountain" to share their insights with the larger society.

To experience the deepest truths of their own humanity, seers have always sought the seclusion of nature. And the natural world, that wondrous field that gave birth to human consciousness, has yielded insights into the nature of who we are.

Some writers suggest that the beginnings of religious practice, the roots of meditation, may find their origin in the stillness of mind practiced by ancient hunters as they waited for their quarry. The first traces of religious impulse in human prehistory came to light in a cave in the Swiss Alps. There, more than 40,000 years ago, our ancestors arranged bear skulls and bones ritually in stone crypts. European cave art from around that time elegantly depict a mix of natural and supernatural creatures reverently painted on the walls of inner chambers. From our earliest days as humans, our species has gleaned its most vibrant truths from the natural world. Like Plato, we have looked into and through the outward forms of nature to a deeper context where the mysteries of existence -- of life, birth and death, and what may lie beyond them -- are glimpsed.

Closer to our own time, the great naturalist Charles Darwin pondered the wonders he encountered on the Galapagos Islands, where a dozen species of finches were perfectly adapted to fit a range of diverse habitats. In his journal he wrote: "One could presume from an original paucity of birds on this archipelago, one species had been taken and modified to different ends." He considered that agent of change over the next half century and eventually brought forth the wisdom of natural selection, one of the the most beautiful and profound secrets of the passage of life on earth.

The poet Mary Oliver writes of this kind of awareness, or attentiveness to nature, as at heart a spiritual act. "This is the first, wildest, and wisest thing I know: that the soul exists, and that it is built entirely out of attentiveness."

* * *

Following his own inner vision, photographer Bruce Heinemann has gathered gems of attentiveness from the world's wisdom traditions. He has selected perspectives on courage, hope, joy enlightenment, faith and love from seers such as Lao-tsu, Jesus, Mahatma Gandhi and Mother Theresa, and paired them with his own striking landscape images. The effect allows these moments of wisdom to open for the reader. But his deeper purpose, I think, is to place these visionary words within a larger context: the beauty of nature, the source of human wisdom.

The "nature of wisdom," as passed down from the oldest of human voices, is to recognize the brevity of our existence, acknowledge our connection with each another and with the rest of life, and to regard each day as the precious and irreplaceable gift it is.

"There are two ways to live your life," Einstein reminds us. "One is as though nothing is a miracle. The other is as though everything is a miracle."

THE EAGLE'S GIFT

I decided that I had better pull off the road to watch the eagle soaring above a ridge before I drove into the snowy hayfield hugging its narrow shoulder. It was a cold morning January in the North Cascades of Washington State. The magnificent bald eagle had caught my eye several miles back as he glided effortlessly hundreds of feet above the glistening pasture, then descended abruptly, almost seeming to follow along as I wound my way around each bend and turn in the road. As much as I am fascinated by them, I had never really made much effort to photograph bald eagles, but I thought maybe this one had seen fit to join me for some reason. I quickly pulled my camera gear out of the van and began to set my tripod; I hoped to catch at least one shot before he decided to fly off. To my surprise, he seemed in no hurry to go anywhere as he lazily circled the field. It had been less than six months since I had quit my part-time job to pursue my passion as a nature photographer, and hardly a day had passed that I didn't find myself worrying about how I was actually going to make a living doing fine art landscape photography. The world was full of nature photographers and ex-photographers who couldn't make it a living, and I constantly asked myself, "How was I going to make it?"

As I began to follow him in my lens, adjusting the focus to grab a shot, I became mesmerized, almost hypmotized, by the gently undulating motion of his dips and graceful turns. All the airspace in view was his personal playground. I stopped tracking him in the lens and simply observed him, unable to take my eyes off him. In this attentive moment I completely forgot about photographing him, allowing myself to for a moment become that eagle, utterly free and unencumbered by human thought and experience. What must it be like wake every morning, take flight above all creation and not worry about how it was going to feed itself that day? Rather, simply to be, to do what it has always done, to trust and follow its instincts, and simply let nature provide. I took my eyes off him for a moment as I let that idea settle in my conscious mind. Was it possible for me to live my life day to day, knowing and believing deeply like the eagle that I could live as a free spirit, trusting that if I would simply allow myself the courage to pursue my dream, what I desired would come true? After a few minutes, I reclaimed my human impulses and began tracking him again through the lens. I got one shot before he cried out, turned lazily west, and ascended toward the foothills.

That idea rooted itself firmly in my thinking. As I pursued my work- with all of its moments of pleasing successes and deflating failures in the following years-- I strove to keep the spirit of that simple concept in my heart and manifested in my actions. With each new opportunity to photograph the landscape I tried to see ever deeper into the rhythms and patterns of the natural world and discover the processes and structures that speak to us of a higher knowing. It is a journey that has been as challenging as it has been profoundly rewarding.

Several years ago I was working on a book and music CD soundtrack about the American landscape which included imagery from the Desert Southwest. In preparation for an arduous six day photo journey through the Escalante River Canyon, I decided that, as I was 49 years old, a physical exam would be in order. I had kept myself in great shape since high school, running and lifting weights, so I assumed I would pass with no problem. At the reading of my lab results, the doctor's face turned red as he looked me in the eye and said it was likely that I had prostate cancer. This was later confirmed by a biopsy. I was utterly stunned. How could this possibly happen to me? It was a very long month between diagnosis and my surgery to remove the prostate gland. Although many men eventually get prostate cancer, it is particularly dangerous to men under 50 years of age as it tends to be quite aggressive at that age, with a corresponding poorer prognosis. I had so much to think about. My daughter was sixteen and my son was nine. I laid awake almost every night pondering the frightening thought of my children going on in their life without their father.

As I had done so often in the past when the stress and challenges of life build up, I gathered up my camera gear and headed out into the natural world, seeking comfort, clarity, and insight. This time it was different, however, because my cancer brought a new perspective and context to everything in my life. Standing on a rock outcropping one evening, gazing at the San Juan Islands stretched out before me in the warm light of the setting sun, a bald eagle, hovering in gentle updrafts of the nearby cliffs, caught my attention. Again, as I had done years before in that snowy field in the North Cascades, I put my camera aside one more time and became transfixed on this marvel of nature.

Finding a comfortable patch of grass to rest in, I leaned back against the mossy hillside, keeping my attention focused on the eagle as he seemed to float across the face of the cliff. Each subtle movement and change of direction so smooth, it was as if his actions were simply a thought in his mind. If only it was that easy for our species, I mused. The eagle dropped abruptly, turned sharply to the left, and disappeared around the side of the cliff.

All of a sudden I was alone, with only that notion fresh in my consciousness. The view before me became a blur as I was now completely lost in the contemplation of this simple idea. In this quiet moment, I was reminded of the words of two great spiritual masters, for it was Jesus who said, "As a man thinketh, so he is.", and in the teachings of Buddha, "We are what we think. All that we are arises with our thoughts. With our thoughts we make the world." This I already knew. But as is so often the story in our lives, we allow our spirit to be trampled and diminished by the daily challenges of living. Living free requires that we refresh and revitalize our belief and understanding of these simple truths. I asked myself, "What other values and ideas about living have I forgotten or perhaps never known?" It was something I decided I wanted to explore. As I had found so many times before, in nature there is a wisdom and knowing, sometimes literal sometimes metaphorical, that would make it the perfect vehicle for this journey of discovery. I would put aside my current book project and make this idea my next book. As I got up to leave, a piercing cry shattered the silence. The eagle ascended rapidly from the cliff beneath me. Looking down at me, he paused momentarily before he banked slowly in a gradual arc and headed out over the water. I stood and followed him until his dark form melted into the silhouette of Burrows Island.

In the two years that followed that transformative moment I spent much time reading and seeking out the teachings and wisdom of some of the greatest literary, scientific, and spiritual masters of all time. Some ideas and notions I was already familiar with, but many were revelations, or perhaps simply things that I was seeing anew, with fresh eyes, as my experience with cancer had so greatly changed the context of how I experienced almost everything in my life. As I compiled the writings from these enlightened people, the themes and ideas they expressed, so common to all human experience, seemed to organize themselves into the six chapters for this book, Courage, Hope, Joy, Enlightenment, Faith, and Love. The process was not just illuminating. More than that, it was a true affirmation for me of the extraordinary richness that life offers and the almost unfathomable potential we all possess to create love and happiness in our own lives.

When I set out to photograph for the book, one Zen saying stayed with me, "Every step of the journey is the journey." And while I had always tried to approach each day I spent photographing as an entirely unique and complete experience, the presence of cancer in my life created a much deeper and more profound meaning of one whole day. As I continued to photograph, I found myself beginning to think of each day not as a day in my life, but each day ***as my life***. I began to think of my life as an ever-evolving musical score. Each day another opportunity for a new performance, a chance to enrich the composition with ever greater complexity and expression, with a growing maturity and grace that only life's experience can provide. I came to realize that all we are ever given is the gift of a new day, and what we choose to do with that gift are simply the notes and measures that compose the symphony of our life.

It has now been three years since my surgical treatment and I am in remission, although I still have another three years of monitoring before I am declared cured. This book project has been an enormously cathartic experience for me. I feel fortunate indeed that I have had the opportunity to use my art as a means of facing and exploring such a challenge. My hope is that you will find in the following pages images of our world and expressions of a higher order that will give you comfort and perhaps even inspire a deeper appreciation of your life and the greater potential that it offers. Life is a gift, and the best way to honor that gift is to, like the eagle, simply take wing and fly.

DEDICATED

to all who live with

love and compassion,

for they are

the peacemakers

and shall inherit the earth.

The Nature of Wisdom

‹ COURAGE ›

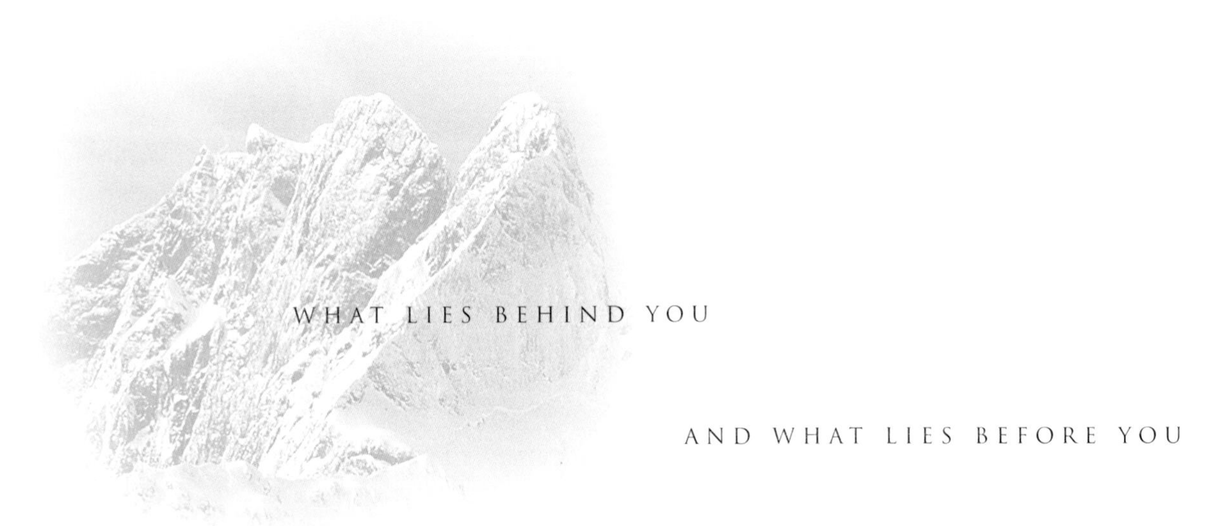

WHAT LIES BEHIND YOU

AND WHAT LIES BEFORE YOU

ARE TINY MATTERS COMPARED

TO WHAT LIES WITHIN YOU.

· RALPH WALDO EMERSON ·

· COURAGE ·

DO NOT GO WHERE THE PATH MAY LEAD,

GO INSTEAD

WHERE THERE IS NO PATH AND

LEAVE A TRAIL.

· RALPH WALDO EMERSON ·

· C O U R A G E ·

A JOURNEY

OF A THOUSAND MILES

MUST BEGIN WITH

A SINGLE STEP.

· LAO-TZU ·

·COURAGE·

GENIUS IS FORMED IN QUIET,

CHARACTER

IN THE STREAM OF LIFE.

· GOETHE ·

·COURAGE·

HAVE COURAGE FOR THE GREAT SORROWS OF LIFE

AND PATIENCE FOR THE SMALL ONES;

AND WHEN YOU HAVE LABORIOUSLY

ACCOMPLISHED YOUR DAILY TASK,

GO TO SLEEP IN PEACE.

GOD IS AWAKE.

· VICTOR HUGO ·

· COURAGE ·

TO KEEP OUR FACES TOWARD CHANGE AND

BEHAVE LIKE FREE SPIRITS

IN THE PRESENCE OF FATE

IS STRENGTH UNDEFEATABLE.

· HELEN KELLER ·

· C O U R A G E ·

VITALITY SHOWS

NOT ONLY IN THE

ABILITY TO PERSIST,

BUT IN THE ABILITY TO START OVER.

· F. SCOTT FITZGERALD ·

· COURAGE ·

ZEAL IS THE VOLCANO,

THE PEAK OF WHICH

THE GRASS OF INDECISIVENESS

DOES NOT GROW.

· KAHLIL GIBRAN ·

· COURAGE ·

YOU SHALL BE FREE

INDEED WHEN YOUR DAYS

ARE NOT WITHOUT A CARE NOR YOUR NIGHTS

WITHOUT A WANT AND A GRIEF.

BUT RATHER WHEN THESE THINGS GIRDLE YOUR LIFE

AND YET YOU RISE ABOVE THEM

NAKED AND UNBOUND.

· KAHLIL GIBRAN ·

· C O U R A G E ·

WHATEVER YOU CAN DO,

OR BELIEVE YOU CAN DO, BEGIN IT,

FOR BOLDNESS HAS GENIUS,

POWER, AND MAGIC IN IT.

· GOETHE ·

· C O U R A G E ·

COURAGE IS RIGHTLY ESTEEMED

THE FIRST OF HUMAN QUALITIES

BECAUSE IT IS THE QUALITY WHICH

GUARANTEES ALL OTHERS.

· WINSTON CHURCHILL ·

· COURAGE ·

The Nature of Wisdom

~ Hope ~

IN EVERY WINTER'S HEART

THERE IS A

QUIVERING SPRING,

AND BEHIND THE VEIL OF EACH NIGHT

THERE IS A SMILING DAWN.

· KAHLIL GIBRAN ·

~ *Hope* ~

THE BEST REASON FOR

HAVING DREAMS

IS THAT IN DREAMS

NO REASONS ARE NECESSARY.

· ASHLEIGH BRILLIANT ·

~ Hope ~

YESTERDAY IS A DREAM,

TOMORROW BUT A VISION.

BUT TODAY WELL LIVED MAKES EVERY YESTERDAY

A DREAM OF HAPPINESS,

AND EVERY TOMORROW A VISION OF HOPE.

LOOK WELL, THEREFORE TO THIS DAY.

· SANSKRIT PROVERB ·

Hope

IN THE HOUR OF ADVERSITY

BE NOT

WITHOUT

HOPE.

FOR CRYSTAL RAIN FALLS

FROM BLACK CLOUDS.

· PERSIAN POEM ·

~ Hope ~

CHARACTER

MAY BE MANIFESTED

IN THE GREAT MOMENTS,

BUT IT IS MADE

IN THE SMALL ONES.

· WINSTON CHURCHILL ·

~ Hope ~

TO KNOW HOW

TO GROW OLD

IS THE MASTERWORK OF WISDOM,

AND ONE OF THE MOST DIFFICULT

CHAPTERS IN THE GREAT ART OF LIVING.

· HENRI FREDERIC AMIEL ·

~ Hope ~

MAY THE STARS CARRY YOUR SADNESS AWAY.

MAY THE FLOWERS

FILL YOUR HEART WITH BEAUTY.

AND MAY HOPE FOREVER

WIPE AWAY YOUR TEARS.

· CHIEF DAN GEORGE ·

~ Hope ~

BEAUTY IS TRUTH,

TRUTH BEAUTY –

THAT IS ALL YE KNOW ON EARTH

AND ALL YE NEED TO KNOW.

· JOHN KEATS ·

~ *Hope* ~

EACH SECOND YOU CAN BE REBORN.

EACH SECOND THERE CAN BE

A NEW BEGINNING.

IT IS CHOICE.

IT IS YOUR CHOICE.

· CLEARWATER ·

Hope

THE GEM CANNOT BE POLISHED

WITHOUT FRICTION NOR

MAN PERFECTED WITHOUT TRIALS.

· CHINESE PROVERB ·

~ Hope ~

THE TIMELESS IN YOU IS AWARE OF

LIFE'S TIMELESSNESS;

AND KNOWS THAT YESTERDAY

IS BUT TODAY'S MEMORY

AND TOMORROW IS TODAY'S DREAM.

· KAHLIL GIBRAN ·

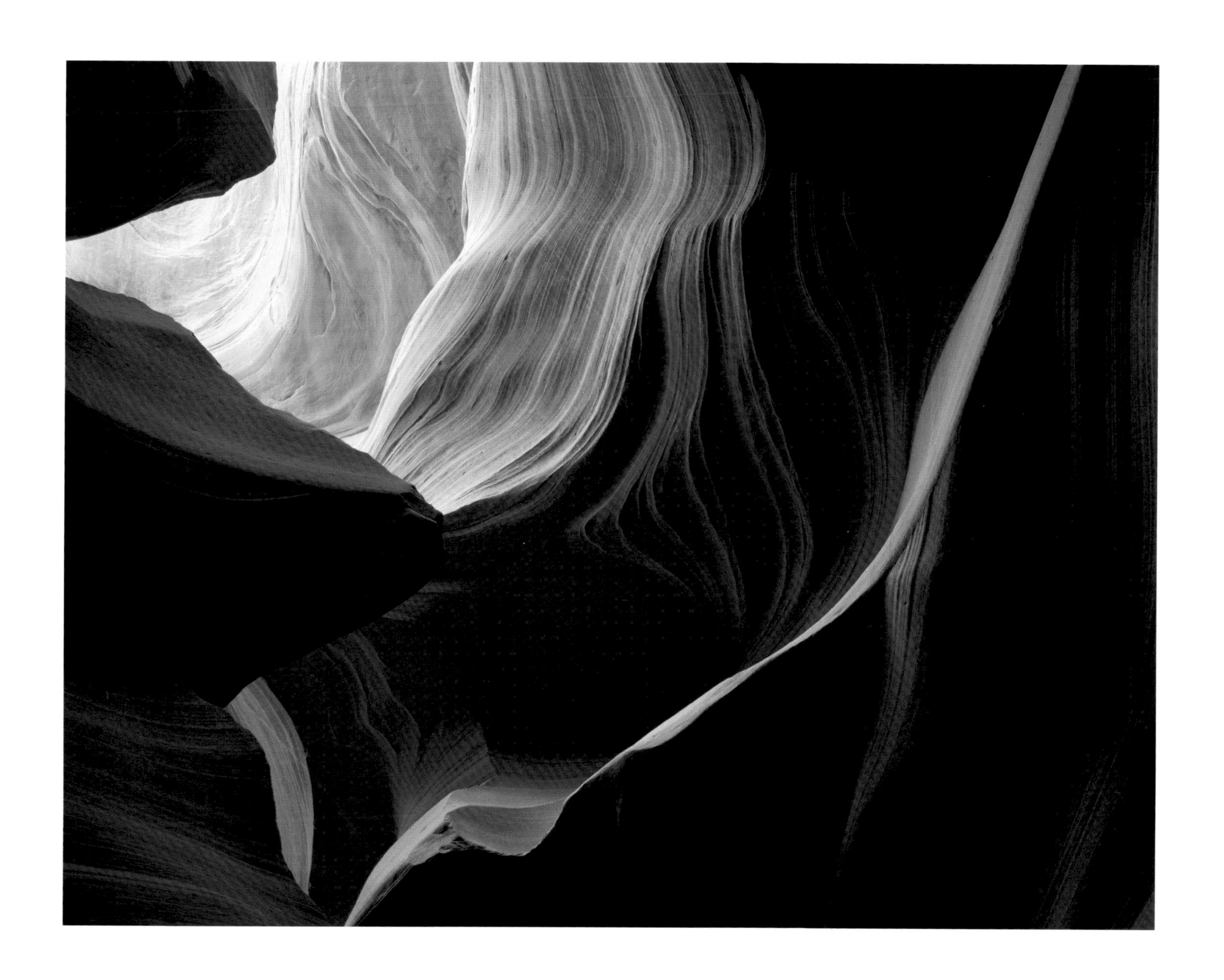

Hope

The Nature of Wisdom

Joy

AND BEAUTY IS NOT A NEED BUT AN ECSTASY.

IT IS NOT A MOUTH THIRSTING NOR AN EMPTY HAND

STRETCHED FORTH, BUT RATHER

A HEART ENFLAMED AND A SOUL ENCHANTED.

BEAUTY IS ETERNITY GAZING AT ITSELF IN A MIRROR.

BUT YOU ARE ETERNITY AND YOU ARE THE MIRROR.

· KAHLIL GIBRAN ·

Joy

THE MASTER IN THE ART OF LIVING

MAKES LITTLE DISTINCTION BETWEEN HIS WORK AND HIS PLAY,

HIS LABOR AND HIS LEISURE,

HIS MIND AND HIS BODY,

HIS EDUCATION AND HIS RECREATION,

HIS LOVE AND HIS RELIGION.

HE HARDLY KNOWS WHICH IS WHICH.

HE SIMPLY PURSUES HIS VISION

OF EXCELLENCE IN WHATEVER HE DOES,

LEAVING OTHERS TO DECIDE WHETHER HE IS WORKING

OR PLAYING. TO HIM HE IS ALWAYS DOING BOTH.

· ZEN BUDDHIST TEXT ·

Joy

YES, THERE IS A NIRVANA:

IT IS IN LEADING YOUR SHEEP

TO A GREEN PASTURE,

AND IN PUTTING YOUR CHILD TO SLEEP,

AND IN WRITING THE LAST LINE OF YOUR POEM.

· KAHLIL GIBRAN ·

Joy

WRITE IN YOUR

HEART THAT

EVERY DAY IS THE BEST DAY

OF THE YEAR.

· RALPH WALDO EMERSON ·

Joy

YOU PRAY IN YOUR DISTRESS

AND IN YOUR NEED:

WOULD THAT YOU MIGHT PRAY ALSO IN THE

FULLNESS OF YOUR JOY

AND IN YOUR DAYS OF ABUNDANCE.

FOR WHAT IS PRAYER BUT THE EXPANSION OF

YOURSELF INTO THE LIVING ETHER?

· KAHLIL GIBRAN ·

Joy

DRINK DEEPLY.

LIVE IN SERENITY

AND JOY.

· BUDDHA ·

Joy

IF WHAT'S IN YOUR DREAMS

WASN'T ALREADY

INSIDE OF YOU

HOW COULD YOU EVEN DREAM IT?

· KOBI YAMADA ·

Joy

EVERY STEP

OF THE JOURNEY

IS THE JOURNEY.

· ZEN SAYING ·

Joy

LIFE ISN'T ABOUT FINDING YOURSELF.

LIFE IS ABOUT

CREATING YOURSELF.

· UNKNOWN ·

Joy

DANCE LIKE NO ONE IS WATCHING.

SING LIKE NO ONE IS LISTENING.

LOVE LIKE YOU'VE NEVER BEEN HURT AND

LIVE LIKE ITS HEAVEN ON EARTH.

· WILLIAM PURKEY ·

Joy

LIFE IS NOT ABOUT

THE BREATHS YOU TAKE;

IT IS ABOUT THE

MOMENTS

THAT TAKE YOUR BREATH AWAY.

· UNKNOWN ·

Joy

The Nature of Wisdom

‹ ENLIGHTENMENT ›

A MOMENT'S INSIGHT

IS SOMETIMES

WORTH A LIFE'S

EXPERIENCE.

· OLIVER WENDELL HOLMES ·

· ENLIGHTENMENT ·

THREE THINGS

CANNOT BE LONG HIDDEN:

THE SUN, THE MOON,

AND THE TRUTH.

· BUDDHA ·

· ENLIGHTENMENT ·

IMAGINATION IS THE BEGINNING OF CREATION.

YOU IMAGINE WHAT YOU DESIRE.

YOU WILL WHAT YOU IMAGINE AND AT LAST YOU

CREATE WHAT YOU WILL.

· GEORGE BERNARD SHAW ·

· ENLIGHTENMENT ·

WE ARE WHAT WE THINK.

ALL THAT WE ARE ARISES

WITH OUR THOUGHTS

WITH OUR THOUGHTS WE MAKE THE WORLD.

· BUDDHA ·

· ENLIGHTENMENT ·

A PROBLEM CANNOT BE SOLVED

AT THE SAME

LEVEL OF CONSCIOUSNESS

IN WHICH IT WAS CREATED.

· ALBERT EINSTEIN ·

· ENLIGHTENMENT ·

WE CANNOT ONLY LIVE FOR OURSELVES.

A THOUSAND FIBERS CONNECT US

WITH OUR FELLOW MAN:

AND ALONG THOSE FIBERS,

AS SYMPATHETIC THREADS,

OUR ACTIONS RUN AS CAUSES,

AND THEY COME BACK TO US AS EFFECTS.

· MELVILLE ·

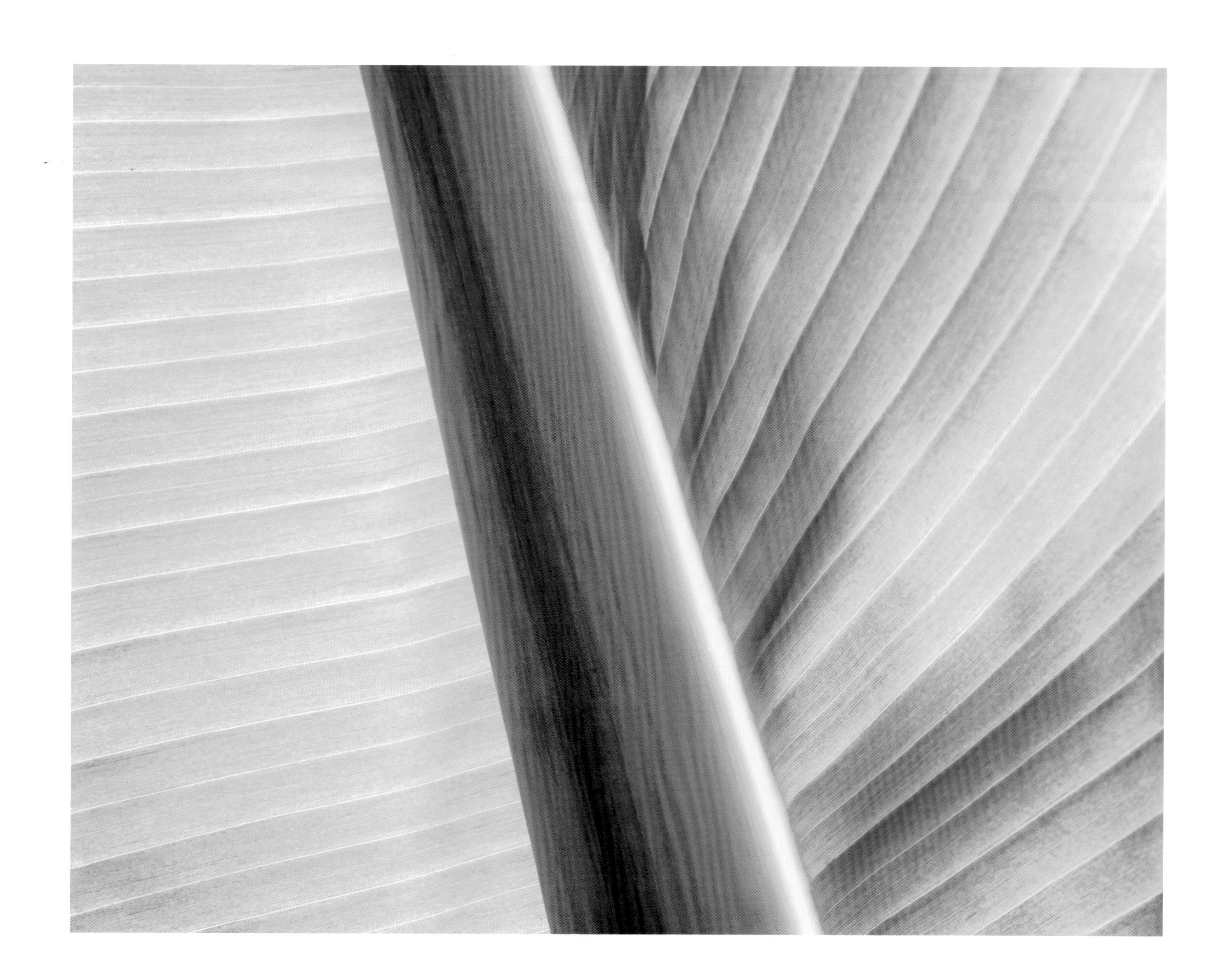

· ENLIGHTENMENT ·

TO A MIND THAT IS STILL

THE WHOLE UNIVERSE

SURRENDERS.

· CHANG TZU ·

· ENLIGHTENMENT ·

IT IS

THE PRIVILEGE

OF WISDOM

TO LISTEN.

· OLIVER WENDELL HOLMES ·

· ENLIGHTENMENT ·

IN THE ATTITUDE OF

SILENCE THE SOUL

FINDS THE PATH IN

A CLEARER LIGHT,

AND WHAT IS ELUSIVE AND DECEPTIVE RESOLVES ITSELF

INTO CRYSTAL CLEARNESS.

OUR LIFE IS A LONG AND ARDUOUS QUEST

AFTER TRUTH.

· MAHATMA GANDHI ·

· ENLIGHTENMENT ·

BE THE

CHANGE

YOU WANT TO SEE

IN THE WORLD

· MAHATMA GANDHI ·

· ENLIGHTENMENT ·

WE ARE FORMED AND MOLDED

BY OUR THOUGHTS.

THOSE WHOSE MINDS ARE SHAPED BY

SELFLESS THOUGHTS GIVE JOY

WHEN THEY SPEAK OR ACT.

JOY FOLLOWS THEM LIKE A SHADOW

THAT NEVER LEAVES THEM.

· BUDDHA ·

· ENLIGHTENMENT ·

The Nature of Wisdom

~ Faith ~

TO EXIST IS TO CHANGE.

TO CHANGE IS TO MATURE;

TO MATURE IS TO GO ON

CREATING ONESELF ENDLESSLY.

· HENRI BERGSON ·

Faith

LET US BE LIKE A BIRD FOR A MOMENT,

PERCHED ON A FRAIL BRANCH WHEN HE SINGS;

THOUGH HE FEELS IT BEND,

YET HE SINGS HIS SONGS,

KNOWING THAT HE HAS WINGS.

· VICTOR HUGO ·

~ *Faith* ~

FAITH IS THE

DARING OF THE SOUL

TO GO FARTHER THAN IT CAN SEE.

· ANONYMOUS ·

~ *Faith* ~

BUT IF THESE BEINGS GUARD YOU,

THEY DO SO BECAUSE

THEY HAVE BEEN

SUMMONED BY YOUR PRAYERS.

· ST. AMBROSE ·

~ *Faith* ~

THERE ARE TWO WAYS TO LIVE YOUR LIFE.

ONE IS AS THOUGH NOTHING IS A MIRACLE.

THE OTHER IS AS THOUGH

EVERYTHING IS A MIRACLE.

· ALBERT EINSTEIN ·

Faith

FOR WHAT IS IT TO DIE BUT TO STAND NAKED IN THE WIND

AND TO MELT INTO THE SUN? AND WHAT IS TO CEASE BREATHING,

BUT TO FREE THE BREATH FROM ITS RESTLESS TIDES, THAT IT MAY

RISE AND EXPAND AND SEEK GOD UNENCUMBERED?

ONLY WHEN YOU DRINK FROM THE RIVER OF SILENCE SHALL YOU INDEED SING.

AND WHEN YOU HAVE REACHED

THE MOUNTAIN TOP, THEN YOU SHALL BEGIN TO CLIMB.

AND WHEN THE EARTH SHALL CLAIM YOUR LIMBS,

THEN SHALL YOU TRULY DANCE.

· KAHLIL GIBRAN ·

~ Faith ~

BETWEEN US AND THE STARS,

THERE LIES BUT SILENCE;

AND THERE IN THE STILLNESS

LET US LISTEN TO THE

VOICE THAT IS SPEAKING WITHIN US.

· JEROME K. JEROME ·

~ *Faith* ~

FOLLOW YOUR

DREAMS.

THEY

KNOW THE WAY.

· KOBI YAMADA ·

~ *Faith* ~

THERE IS

ONE THING ALONE

THAT STANDS THE BRUNT OF LIFE

THROUGHOUT ITS COURSE:

A QUIET CONSCIENCE.

· EURIPIDES ·

~ *Faith* ~

YOUR VISION

WILL BECOME ONLY WHEN YOU

LOOK INTO YOUR HEART.

WHO LOOKS OUTSIDE, DREAMS.

WHO LOOKS INSIDE, AWAKENS.

· CARL JUNG ·

~ *Faith* ~

YOU ARE NOT ENCLOSED

WITHIN YOUR BODIES,

NOR CONFINED TO HOUSES OR FIELDS.

THAT WHICH IS YOU DWELLS

ABOVE THE MOUNTAIN AND

ROVES WITH THE WIND.

· KAHLIL GIBRAN ·

Faith

The Nature of Wisdom

~ Love ~

HE ALONE IS GREAT WHO TURNS THE

VOICE OF THE WIND

INTO A SONG

MADE SWEETER BY HIS OWN LOVING.

· KAHLIL GIBRAN ·

Love

TO LOVE AND BE LOVED

IS TO FEEL THE SUN

FROM BOTH SIDES.

· DAVID VISCOTT ·

Love

I OFFER YOU PEACE. I OFFER YOU LOVE.

I OFFER YOU FRIENDSHIP. I SEE YOUR BEAUTY.

I HEAR YOUR NEED.

I FEEL YOUR FEELINGS. MY WISDOM

FLOWS FROM THE HIGHEST SOURCE.

I SALUTE THAT SOURCE IN YOU.

LET US WORK TOGETHER FOR UNITY AND LOVE.

· MAHATMA GANDHI ·

Love

YOUR FRIEND IS YOUR NEEDS ANSWERED.

HE IS YOUR FIELD WHICH YOU SOW WITH LOVE

AND REAP WITH THANKSGIVING

AND IN THE SWEETNESS OF FRIENDSHIP

LET THERE BE LAUGHTER, AND SHARING OF PLEASURES.

FOR IN THE DEW OF LITTLE THINGS

THE HEART FINDS ITS MORNING

AND IS REFRESHED.

· KAHLIL GIBRAN ·

Love

FOR TRUE LOVE IS INEXHAUSTIBLE;

THE MORE YOU GIVE,

THE MORE YOU HAVE.

AND IF YOU GO TO DRAW AT THE TRUE FOUNTAINHEAD,

THE MORE WATER YOU DRAW,

THE MORE ABUNDANT IS ITS FLOW.

· MAHATMA GANDHI ·

Love

ONE KIND WORD

CAN WARM

THREE WINTER MONTHS.

· JAPANESE PROVERB ·

Love

THOUSANDS OF CANDLES

CAN BE LIGHTED

FROM A SINGLE CANDLE,

AND THE LIFE OF THE CANDLE

WILL NOT BE SHORTENED.

HAPPINESS NEVER DECREASES BY

BEING SHARED.

· MAHATMA GANDHI ·

Love

WHO TRAVELS

FOR LOVE

FINDS A THOUSAND MILES

NOT LONGER THAN ONE.

· JAPANESE PROVERB ·

Love

HE WHO IS IN LOVE IS WISE

AND IS BECOMING WISER,

SEES NEWLY EVERY TIME HE LOOKS

AT THE OBJECT BELOVED,

DRAWING FROM IT WITH HIS EYES AND HIS MIND THOSE

VIRTUES WHICH IT POSSESSES.

· RALPH WALDO EMERSON ·

Love

ALL LOVE IS SWEET,

GIVEN OR RETURNED.

COMMON AS LIGHT IS LOVE,

AND ITS FAMILIAR VOICE WEARIES NOT EVER....

THEY WHO INSPIRE IT MOST ARE FORTUNATE,

AS I AM NOW;

BUT THOSE WHO FEEL IT MOST ARE

HAPPIER STILL.

· PERCY BYSSHE SHELLEY ·

Love

KIND WORDS

CAN BE SHORT

AND EASY TO SPEAK,

BUT THEIR ECHOES

ARE ENDLESS.

· MOTHER TERESA ·

Love

NOTES ON PHOTOGRAPHY

It was the late renowned photographer, Ernst Haas, once considering the relationship between the photographer's creative impulse and their emotions, who observed, "The eye is the lens of the heart". Photography is "The Art of Seeing", and in order to see, one must feel or respond to a sense of connectedness to the subject It has also been said that often times a photograph can reveal as much about the person behind the camera as the subject in front of it. What we choose to photograph and how we ultimately render it as an image, reveals most of all, those things in our world whose virtues and qualities to which we are irresistibly drawn.

I like to think of my approach to photographing as a free-form jazz composition. I plan my trips to places based not so much upon landmarks or regions, but more by what forms, textures, patterns, colors, light, and weather exist there. This idea is the basic compositional form of the trip, as it were. Within that form, I simply wander, letting myself be lured to a distant horizon where the rain is falling, or perhaps following a dry wash up a desert canyon to see what marvels of forms and colors the passing of millions of years have left in the Kayenta sandstone walls. The joys and, indeed the rewards, of landscape photography lay in the discovery of familiar subjects seen in a new light or time of year, or those things come upon for the first time that simply take your breath away. It is the unending and infinite visual and experiential possibilities of photographing nature from which arises the vitality and profoundly expressive potential of this artform.

Although some of the images in this book were taken before I conceived of the idea, most of them were captured with The Nature of Wisdom concept in mind. I set about to photograph for the book not trying to get specific pictures for particular quotes. Rather, I tried to keep the six themes in mind and simply let my eye and heart take me where they would, drawing me to scenes or subject matter that possessed notably expressive or metaphorical content. As I was working on this project, I often mused that I was proving the converse of the old saying, "One picture worth a thousand words"; that is, "one idea or sentiment clearly expressed may find voice in a thousand different images." While I believe this to be true, I unfortunately had to edit from many hundreds of worthy images to create the relative few in this collection that ultimately appear in the book.

Most of the images in this book were taken using either a Pentax 67 format camera or a Nikon 35mm camera system using Fuji Velvia Film. On the following pages are noted the locations and equipment used to capture the image listed. In those few instances where Velvia film was not used, the film used is noted. In September of 2003, I, with much excitement and anticipation, sold all of my film cameras and made the transition to digital capture, acquiring a Canon EOS 1DS, 11 mega-pixel camera. It did not take more than a brief afternoon shooting autumn forests along Stevens Pass Highway in Washington State to see what an enormous improvement digital capture is over film based photography. The digital image has a greater dynamic range, allowing for the representation of brighter highlights and deeper shadows together in the same image. Also quite noticeable is the very smooth gradation of tones and the virtual absence of grain, which is such an inherent detraction in film. And finally, I have found the resolution to equal or exceed the medium format Pentax 67 system that I had used for so many years. For those of you so inclined, you may wish to compare the digital images in this book with the ones captured on film.

All of the images in this book are available as fine art, archival prints. For more information, you may contact Bruce W. Heinemann at: (360)588-8188.
To view more of his images and to get information about his fine art corporate calendar offerings, please visit his website at: www.theartofnature.com.

PHOTOGRAPHIC PLATES

85 Monoliths in Sunset, Bandon Oregon. Wisner Expedition 4X5, Rodenstock 240mm lens.

87 Sunset over The Grand Canyon, Arizona. Canon EOS 1DS, 24-70mm zoom lens.

89 Frost on My Living Room Window, Washington. Nikon FE-2, 70-200mm zoom lens. Kodachrome 25.

91 Escalante River Canyon, Utah. Pentax 67, 135mm lens.

93 Fire and Ice, Straits of Juan De Fuca, Washington. Nikon FE, 70-200mm lens. Kodachrome 25.

95 Autumn Pond Abstract, Upstate New York. Nikon FM2, 70-300mm zoom lens.

97 Blooming Redbud in Spring Forest, Tennessee. Canon EOS 1DS, 70-200mm zoom lens.

99 Autumn Maple Trees, New Hampshire. Pentax 67, 135mm lens.

101 Banana Leaf Design, Washington. Pentax 67, 135mm lens.

103 Winter Aspen Abstract, Methow Valley, Washington. Pentax 67, 135mm lens.

105 Early Spring, Skate Creek, Washington. Pentax 67, 135mm lens.

107 Sierra Nevada Mountains, Lone Pine, California. Pentax 67, 135mm lens.

109 Autumn Portrait, North Cascades, Washington. Pentax 67, 200mm lens.

111 Long Canyon, Grand Escalante Staricase, Utah. Canon EOS 1DS, 70-200mm zoom lens.

113 Multnomah Falls, Columbia River Gorge, Oregon. Pentax 67, 200mm lens.

115 Autumn Maple in Fog, Blue Ridge Parkway, North Carolina. Pentax 67, 135mm lens.

117 Bird Silhouette, Washington. Nikon FE2, 70-200mm zoom lens. Kodachrome 25.

119 Autumn Forest in Fog, Blue Ridge Parkway, North Carolina. Pentax 67, 135mm lens.

121 Autumn Aspen Forest, Steamboat Springs, Colorado. Pentax 67, 135mm lens.

123 Grand Teton Mountains in Breaking Fog, Teton National Park. Nikon FM2, 70-300mm zoom lens.

125 Sunset over San Juan Islands from Mt. Erie, Anacortes, Washington. Pentax 67, 200mm lens.

127 Moonset over Monument Valley, Utah. Nikon FM2, 70-300mm zoom lens.

129 Misty Autumn Creek, Stevens Pass, Washington. Canon EOS 1DS, 24-70mm zoom lens.

131	Eagle Falls, Stevens Pass, Washington. Canon EOS 1DS, 24-70mm zoom lens.
133	Cottonwood Tree in Sunlight, Long Canyon, Grand Escalante Staircase, Utah. Canon EOS 1DS, 24-70mm zoom lens.
135	Breaking Thunderstorm over Priest Lake, Idaho. Nikon FM2, 70-300mm zoom lens.
137	Wildflower Bouquet, Washington. Nikon FM, 70-300mm zoom lens with extension tube.
139	Autumn Pasture, Swan Valley, Idaho. Pentax 67, 135mm lens.
141	New Zealand Flax, Washington. Nikon FM2, 70-300mm lens with extension tube.
143	Bash Bish Falls, New York State. Pentax 67, 90mm lens.
145	Rattlesnake Grass in Morning Dew, Occidental, California. Nikon FM2, 70-300mm zoom lens with extension tube.
147	Falls Creek Falls, Idaho. Pentax 67, 135mm lens.
149	Winter Apple Orchard, Wenatchee, Washington. Nikon FE2, 80-200mm zoom lens, Kodachrome 25.
151	Frosted Pine Trees, Leavenworth, Washington. Nikon FE2, 80-200mm zoom lens.
153	Sunset, White Sands National Monument, New Mexico. Pentax 67, 135mm lens.
155	Iris and Lilypads, Washington. Nikon FE2, 70-300mm zoom lens.
157	Rhododendrons in Cedar Forest, Washington. Pentax 67, 135mm lens.
159	St Mary's Lake, Glacier National Park, Montana. Pentax 67, 135mm lens.
160	Autumn Aspens, Stevens Pass Highway, Washington. Canon EOS 1DS, 70-200mm zoom lens.
167	Late Spring Evening in the Palouse Hills, Eastern Washington. Canon EOS 1DS, 70-200mm zoom lens.

BRUCE W. HEINEMANN

American landscape photographer, Bruce W. Heinemann, has photographed the landscape for over twenty five years. He is the photographer of the critically-acclaimed, best-selling book, The Art of Nature: Reflections of the Grand Design. He also authored and photographed a second best-selling book, A Guide to Photographing the Art of Nature. Both books were Book of the Month Club Feature Selections. He was also the photographer and author of a photographic book on his native state entitled, Washington: A Gallery of the Seasons. His most recent publication, The Four Seasons book and music CD has met with great acclaim.

His images have appeared in Sierra Magazine, Audubon, Outdoor Photographer, Alaska Airlines, and National Geographic, among others. He was a cinamatographer and co-producer of a video entitled, The Art of Nature: Reflections on the Grand Design, based on his book, and narrated by Emmy-winning actor, Tom Skerritt. It received The Gold Award at the 1996 Houston International Film Festival for best music video, and was broadcast on over 140 Public Television Stations in the United States.

In 1993 he was the recipient of the Virginia Merrill Bloedel Lecture Fellow Award, given to recognize and promote the accomplishments of individuals who have contributed to the welfare of nature.

He has photographed and published fine art corporate calendars for over eighteen years. Among his clients are national corporations from many sectors of business including pharmaceutical, insurance, real estate, and financial institutions, among others. His images are also included in many private and corporate collections as well as represented by several fine art galleries in the United States. He is also an accomplished classical/jazz trumpeter.

He lives with his family in the town of Anacortes, on Fidalgo Island, in the San Juan Islands of Washington State.

TO LIVE CONTENT WITH SMALL MEANS; TO SEEK ELEGANCE RATHER THAN LUXURY;
TO STUDY HARD, THINK QUIETLY, TALK GENTLY, ACT FRANKLY; TO LISTEN TO STARS AND BIRDS,
TO BABES AND SAGES, WITH OPEN HEART; TO BEAR ALL CHEERFULLY, DO ALL BRAVELY.
IN A WORD, TO LET THE SPIRITUAL, UNBIDDEN AND UNCONSCIOUS, GROW UP THROUGH THE COMMON.
THIS IS TO BE MY SYMPHONY.

· WILLIAM HENRY CHANNING ·